Original title:
Winter's Icy Embrace

Copyright © 2024 Creative Arts Management OÜ
All rights reserved.

Author: Vivian Laurent
ISBN HARDBACK: 978-9916-94-559-9
ISBN PAPERBACK: 978-9916-94-558-2

Glimmering in the Darkness

Frosty feet in woolen socks,
Penguins slip like silly clocks.
Hot cocoa spills on our warm lap,
While the cat takes an icy nap.

Snowmen dance with carrot noses,
Hats too big, in silly poses.
Chasing flakes like playful mice,
Sure they've gotten way too nice.

Snowflakes' Silent Ballet

Snowflakes twirl and softly shout,
While snowmen pout when they fall out.
Sleds go flying down the hill,
As if they're on a wild thrill.

Laughter echoes through the trees,
Ice skates wobble like pesky bees.
Hot cocoa chugs make kids stampede,
While snowballs fly—oh what a need!

Shadows of the Frosted Pines

Trees wear blankets, all snug and tight,
Squirrels skitter in hilarious flight.
Snow forts double as tiny towers,
Filled with giggles, some silly powers.

Icicles dangle like toothy grins,
While snow angels dance in their spins.
Funny hats on heads so bright,
Playing hide-and-seek by twilight.

A Whisper in the Chill

Chilly breath like little puffs,
Tickling noses, sharing laughs.
Warm hugs wrapped in puffy gear,
As hot soup warms the winter cheer.

Frosted windows tell no lies,
Snowflakes whisper silly sighs.
Bundle up, it's time for play,
Who knew cold could warm the day?

Chilling Embrace of the North

Snowflakes dance without a care,
Frosty breath curls in the air.
Sledding down hills with a squeal,
Hot cocoa's warmth, what a deal!

Sweaters cozy, boots a mess,
Tripping over snow is a test.
Snowmen grin with carrot noses,
In the cold, we find our poses.

Layers of Shimmering Silence

Blankets white on every tree,
Shouts of laughter, can you see?
Snowballs fly with joyful cheer,
Looks like someone's in for a smear!

Footprints lead, then disappear,
Slipping, sliding, tossing cheer.
Hot soup bubbling, what a sight,
Snowflakes twirl in soft moonlight.

The Unfolding of the White Veil

A whistle of chill, the game begins,
Catching snowflakes on our chins.
Frosty noses red and bright,
Chasing snowmen all through the night.

Carving angels with a spin,
Whispered secrets, cozy din.
Games of tag, all in good fun,
Who knew ice could yield this run?

The Icy Kiss of Stillness

Icicles hang like pointy prongs,
Echoes of laughter, winter songs.
Dogs in sweaters tumble around,
Their antics, oh so profound!

Snowflakes land on my warm tea,
Cheeky squirrels dance with glee.
With frozen toes, I jump and shout,
'Who needs summer? Let it sprout!'

Frost-kissed Whispers

The ground is a canvas, all white and bright,
A squirrel in a scarf, what a silly sight!
Snowflakes are gossiping, flurries of cheer,
A snowman's a lawyer, he'll see you right here.

Giggling children with cheeks all aglow,
Slide on the ice like pros in a show.
But someone's stuck, their boots all askew,
While their friends laugh and say, "We'll rescue you too!"

Silent Snowfall Serenade

The flakes fall like feathers, so fluffy and light,
But don't tell the car that it's now out of sight.
A dog in a sweater, all dapper and grand,
Chases its tail, slipping down on the land.

While cocoa is steaming, a marshmallow dive,
Sipping too fast, and oh, look, we arrive!
A giggle erupts as a friend loses grip,
And down they go, like a soft little trip.

The Chill of Solstice Nights

The stars are all twinkling, a crisp velvet veil,
While snowmen debate who's the best at the tale.
Frost on the windows is quite a grand art,
But who drew the mustache? That's the real part!

A penguin in boots takes a stroll down the lane,
With Christmas lights tangled in each little mane.
Hot cider's a treat, though it burns when you sip,
And laughing together, we all start to slip.

Crystal Veils in Twilight

The twilight descends with a magical gleam,
As snowflakes are waltzing, it's all like a dream.
A party of icicles hangs not so straight,
While a cat with a hat feels a bit out of date.

Toboggans are flying, no speed limit near,
While one trips and giggles, "I've lost all my fear!"
With frost on our noses, we savor the fun,
Each chuckle and fall adds to joy, a home run.

The Glistening Pause

The trees are dressed in white,
A snowman's hat takes flight.
With every slip and slide,
We can't help but laugh and bide.

The snowflakes dance like bees,
Tickling our noses with ease.
The ground is a slippery show,
With every tumble, we steal the show.

Hot cocoa spills like a dream,
As kids plot a snowball scheme.
An avalanche of laughter rolls,
In this chilly land, we're all fools.

Frosty hair and cheeks aglow,
We prance like penguins in a row.
With every chuckle shared today,
The cold can't freeze our joyful play.

Tales from the Frozen Lake

On the lake where the ice is thick,
We skate along, trying not to slip.
A game of tag turns into a chase,
When everyone falls with a funny face.

The fishermen freeze, windswept and bold,
As secrets of the lake are humorously told.
A fish jumps high, splashes around,
Synchronized grinning leads to the ground.

Snowmobiles roar like caffeinated bees,
While we glide around with tongue-tied pleas.
With ice that cracks, we jump in surprise,
As skaters spin with peanut-butter eyes.

Hot soup in hand, we stand agape,
At the antics trapped in this icy scrape.
Laughter echoes, no worries in sight,
As we bubble with joy in the frosty light.

Breaths of the Chilling Morning

The dawn unveils a frosty scene,
With frozen noses not so keen.
Every breath puffs like a big balloon,
While squirrels frolic, wearing a raccoon.

Our mittens match, a style unique,
While we munch on snow with a squeak.
The air is crisp, our cheeks turn red,
An adventure wrapped up in laughter instead.

A snowball fight sparks like a flame,
As dodging feels more like a game.
The icy breeze sends shivers through,
Yet joy flutters like a little bluebird too.

With each giggle breaking the freeze,
We create ruckus, such moments please.
We tiptoe out, with hearts so bright,
In this frosty fun, our spirits ignite.

A Canvas of Icebound Quiet

The world outside is painted bright,
With shimmering crystals catching light.
We whisper 'shh', but laughter leaks,
As snowflakes tumble like silly freaks.

Snow forts rise like grandiose dreams,
Built with giggles, the fun redeems.
Who needs a king when we've got snow,
In this frosty kingdom, we steal the show.

The birds are quiet, the trees stand tall,
While we practice our tricks and laugh through it all.
A friendly slip sends us to the ground,
In this hush, our joy is profound.

With snowmen built, our frosty friends,
We toss snow as our laughter never ends.
This canvas quiet may hold its chill,
But we know the warmth of joy at will.

Geometry of Snowflakes

The snowflakes dance like tiny bits,
A geometric mess, each one never fits.
They fall and twirl, oh what a sight,
Like all of them lost in a snowball fight.

My nose is red, my toes go numb,
Laughing at snowmen who look quite dumb.
With carrot noses and twiggy arms,
They stand guard while the hot cocoa warms.

Snowball fights break out with glee,
As children yell, 'You can't hit me!'
But in a flurry, they all bestow,
A face full of powder, time for a glow!

The ground is white, the sky's a mess,
The snowflakes giggle, what a silly dress.
As icicles dangle, ready to drip,
I run away, in an airborne flip!

Kisses from the Icy Blue

Frosty kisses from the chilly air,
My cheeks go pink, but I don't care.
The wind laughs loud, with a cheeky breeze,
Tickling my nose, putting me at ease.

Snowmen wobble, their buttons askew,
While penguins skate, in a funny queue.
If snow could giggle, it would erupt,
At sight of the kids who slip and plump.

Hot chocolate splashes, with marshmallows afloat,
A cozy delight, oh what a cozy note.
As the snowflakes bow and take their leave,
I can't help but smile, oh what a weave!

When the sun peaks in, with a wink in its gleam,
Melting the snowflakes, it's quite the dream.
But the laughter remains, it surely won't fade,
For in icy moments, our giggles parade!

Echoing Silence of the Night

In the hush of night, a snow blanket lies,
While squirrels wear boots, oh what a surprise!
They scurry around, with acorns in tow,
Trying to dance, but they slip on the snow.

The moon peeks in, with a smile so bright,
Casting shadows of snowflakes, oh what a sight!
While snowmen schemed, to share a cold cheer,
They chuckled and swayed, till the kids drew near.

Amidst all the quiet, a snowball lands,
Splat on a snowman, oh what a planned!
With giggles erupting, they scatter like ants,
Oh, the joy of a snow day, and all that it grants!

As the echoes fade, and the stars twinkle bright,
The frosty world dances, filled with delight.
Tomorrow will come, with more snowy sights,
But tonight we giggle, oh what frozen rights!

A Sanctuary of Snow

The snowman wobbles with a grin,
His carrot nose looks slightly thin.
He dances yet with frosty flair,
While squirrels giggle and stare.

The children throw snowballs with glee,
One hits the neighbor's old pine tree.
It shakes and showers snowflakes down,
On the dog who's wearing a frown.

The sleds zoom by, a race of cheer,
One kid yells loudly, "I can steer!"
But that's the moment he takes a spill,
And lands with a thud on the snowy hill.

So grab your gear and join the fun,
In fluffy realms where snowballs run.
For laughter rises in the cold,
Turn up the joy as winter unfolds.

The Depths of Glacier's Heart

The glacier grumbles, quite a sight,
With ice that glimmers in morning light.
It cracks a joke, then takes a bow,
And all the penguins laugh somehow.

The seals have formed a juggling show,
With fish and balls that gleefully flow.
A walrus slips and dashes near,
"Mistakes are fine, just shed a tear!"

The icebergs drift with a jaunty air,
One sports a hat, oh, what a flair!
They tip their caps to boats that pass,
As if to say, "Hey, look! We class!"

With humor bright in chill's embrace,
The frosty world's a laughing place.
So let's join in this icy dance,
And twirl with glee—let's take a chance!

Fables of Evergreen and Ice

The evergreen tree wears snow like a hat,
While rabbits hop, chasing after a cat.
They pause and laugh, then make a pact,
To join in the fun—what a snowy act!

The wise old owl gives a chuckled hoot,
As penguins slide down the pines in pursuit.
It's a slippery race, who will win?
With flippers flailing, they tumble and spin!

A yeti appears, with a grin so wide,
"Wanna join in?" He offers a ride.
But whoops, he slips on his frosty floor,
And the kids erupt in laughter once more.

Fables told with laughter and cheer,
Among the trees, we'll hold them dear.
With snowflakes swirling in silver light,
Let mirth be our guide this chilly night.

The Palette of Cold

The painter captures a scene so bold,
With sprays of white and shades of cold.
Yet the brush slips, in comic flares,
Creating snowmen with funny stares!

The bluebird sings in rhymes so sweet,
While winter's chill gives a chilly greet.
It tries to dance, but slips, oh dear!
A tumble that brings us all to cheer!

The canvas gleams with splashes bright,
A snowball fight, what a sheer delight!
The colors blend, the laughter flows,
In frosty hues, the giggling grows.

So let's create in this chilly dome,
A world of fun where we feel at home.
With colors swirled in laughter's flow,
Let joy be painted—come join the show!

A Shroud of Silence

Snowflakes tumble, soft and white,
Covering all, oh what a sight!
Penguins waddling, in a row,
Slide on ice, then slip—oh no!

Sleds go zooming down the hill,
Screams and laughter, what a thrill!
Hot cocoa spills, marshmallows fly,
Snowman's carrot nose waves goodbye!

Icicles dangle, sharp like swords,
Shovel races, all in hoards!
Frosty breath makes puffs of fun,
Chasing snowballs—everyone runs!

In this frost, the giggles rise,
Silly mittens, no surprise.
Chattering teeth, a dancing cheer,
Oh, this chilly time of year!

The Year's Still, Cold Heart

Trees wear sweaters, snug and tight,
Barking at branches, oh what a sight!
Squirrels dance, quick on their toes,
Planning mischief, as everyone knows.

Frosty air bites at our cheeks,
Funny faces, giddy shrieks!
Snowballs stacked, a fortress tall,
A sudden attack, we might just fall!

Slipping and sliding, that's the game,
Falling down, but all the same—
Laughter rings through frosty air,
Who knew a slip could bring such flair?

So here we gather, full of cheer,
Chasing blizzards, without fear.
Cold as ice, but hearts are warm,
Let's bundle up, escape the harm!

Beneath the Silver Veil

A blanket of snow, so thick and plush,
Hiding the paths, oh what a rush!
Snowmen giggle with buttoned eyes,
As we play tricks, what a surprise!

Cold wind whispers, tickles our nose,
Making us shiver, and strike silly poses.
Under a cloud, the sun plays shy,
Yet snowflakes twirl, dancing on high!

Mittens mismatched, a fashion delight,
Snowflakes land, what a silly flight!
With rosy cheeks and laughter bright,
Winter's cheer fills up the night!

Tumbling down, we fall like leaves,
Laughter erupts—who truly believes?
In this season, we find our jest,
Among the cold, we feel the best!

Lullabies of Frigid Air

The fireplace crackles, a cozy song,
While outside, the wind whistles along.
Blankets piled high, on the couch we nest,
Watching the snow as it flurries a fest.

Socks and slippers, mismatched too,
Tickling toes, what's a girl to do?
Tales of blizzards, stories so wild,
All together, giggling like a child.

Carrots for noses, hats askew,
Frosty fashion, how wonderfully new!
Mittens unite for a snowball fight,
Here in the chill, wrap laughter tight.

So let the snow cover the ground,
With each stumble, joy is found.
As things freeze, let our spirits flare,
Singing softly in the frigid air!

Crystalline Dreams Unfold

Snowflakes dance like drunken bees,
Falling down with such carefree ease.
Kids in suits that puff and pop,
Wobble 'round until they drop.

Sleds become their shiny ships,
Launching off with joyful flips.
But oh! The laughter turns to squeals,
When someone plows into the heels!

Hot cocoa waits but spills instead,
Marshmallows float to greet the spread.
Whipped cream towers lose the fight,
As faces turn to snowy white.

Chasing flakes through swirling air,
Tripping over boots to spare.
In soft and fluffy realms we smile,
Until we slip and flop in style!

Intricacies in Ice

Icicles hang like nature's fangs,
Pointing down like toothy gangs.
Who knew that frozen could be fun?
Unless your tongue was stuck—oh run!

Snowmen stand with crooked grins,
Wearing hats made from old bins.
Carrot noses falling off,
As playful snowballs start to scoff.

Street lamps adorned with icy lace,
Reflect our smiles; what a place!
Yet every step we think we're slick,
Ends with slips and icy tricks.

Cold weather's quirks make us jest,
In a world where frost is best.
So let's embrace the chilly cheer,
With goofy laughter that we hear!

A Canvas of White

A blanket spread on glistening ground,
Where slip and slide is joy unbound.
People leap with gleeful cheers,
While dodging the snowball peers!

Parks transformed with frosty art,
Creative crafts from every heart.
Sledding down a hill too steep,
Who knew falling could bring a leap?

Tights and gloves, mismatched delight,
The perfect style for a snowball fight.
Outrageous outfits dazzle the eye,
Laughter erupts as boomers fly.

Surrounded by this winter flair,
We form our dreams without a care.
With giggles echoing through the nights,
This icy scene ignites delight!

The Touch of Glacial Grace

Frosty fingers tickle our cheeks,
As penguins slide for warmth it seeks.
Snowflakes whisper soft, it's true,
Making dance partners out of two.

The wind plays tricks beneath our hats,
With snowy clumps that chatter like brats.
One tumble down, one graceful spin,
Turned into moments, laughter's kin.

The art of rolling in the snow,
Creates a snow angel, glossy glow.
But watch those flurries, oh so sly,
They might just cuddle you nearby!

So here we are in this chilly place,
With all the charm of frosty grace.
In every slip and joyful chase,
We find our fun in this cold embrace!

Frostbitten Dreams

I woke up with frozen toes,
Chasing warmth where no one goes.
My coffee's cold, just like my feet,
Who knew frostbite could taste so sweet?

My blanket's a igloo, snug and tight,
Penguins slid past, what a funny sight!
Mittens on hands, but still so cold,
I swear my nose just turned to mold!

The dog's in a sweater, looking so grand,
Canines and felines, united we stand.
Snowmen grinning with carrot noses,
Watching us trip while life just dozes.

So let it snow, let it whirl and spin,
A frosty party; let the fun begin.
Dancing with flakes, let's make a scene,
'Cause in this cold, we live like queens!

A Tapestry of Cold Emotions

Frosty windows with shapes that crawl,
I saw a penguin, or was that a mall?
Hot cocoa's steaming with marshmallows bright,
But step outside, it's a snowball fight!

Socks have vanished, slipped out of sight,
To find them is a comical plight.
My ear's a popsicle, frozen for sure,
Watch me strut like a fancy chore!

Snowflakes dance, like feathers of light,
Falling and twirling, what a great sight!
I tripped on a shovel, oh what a show,
Laughter and giggles are all that I know!

With light and joy, the cold we embrace,
Building a snowman, we quicken the pace.
A tapestry woven with colors so bold,
In this chilly world, we're never too cold!

The Hush of Fading Light

Daylight slips like a slippy eel,
Trying to find my nose—what a steal!
The moon's grinning down, all frosty and white,
As I trip on my boots just out of sight.

Hats pulled down low, over my brow,
Feels like I'm wearing a very cold cow.
Stars twinkle softly under blankets of fluff,
Making our hot chocolate seem almost too tough!

I laugh with the snowflakes, they whisper and play,
Chasing each other until the light's gray.
The hush of the dark wrapped tight all around,
Wishing for warmth, but I bounce off the ground!

Candles are flickering, brrr, what a night,
In frozen jest, we beam with delight.
So here we are, famous and bright,
In this fading glow, we'll dance until light!

Icicles' Melancholy Song

Icicles drippin' like nose hairs set free,
Singing sad songs, oh, how can this be?
Bailed out of hot pie, now chillin' with dread,
While snowmen giggle at the things we said.

A frost in my hair makes me look like a queen,
With curls like icicles, you know what I mean!
So I waddled through snow, with boots oh so grand,
Each step a comic adventure unplanned.

Snow forts and bombs, oh, let's start a war,
In this frozen landscape, who could ask for more?
Laughter exploding, with snow in the air,
We'll fight for our rights to chill everywhere!

So hear the song of the sad, icy freeze,
While we stomp through the white with such elegant ease.

Though cold may surround us with melancholy,
Inside we're all warm—quite the funny folly!

Sledding Through Silent Pines

Down the hill with squeals and shouts,
A tumble here, the laughter sprouts.
Snowflakes dance like tiny stars,
As we wipe out, face-first in pars.

Sleds go flying, dogs join the ride,
Snowball fights that cannot hide.
With cheeks aglow and mittens lost,
We race again, no matter the cost.

Kittens peering through the glass,
Watching us, as we fall and pass.
Hot cocoa waits, a sweet delight,
After our snow day, full of fright.

The pines above in glistening coats,
Muffled giggles, all of us goats.
Shoveling snow becomes pure art,
Letting loose, we've stolen the heart.

A Portrait in Pristine White

Blanket soft, all things are still,
A snowman forms, with an orange thrill.
Carrots packed snug for a perfect nose,
While inside we warm, with cocoa flows.

Trees stand tall, in fluffy attire,
I'm stuck in snow, can't get any fire!
The neighbor's cat, so bold and spry,
Pounces on flakes, oh, how they fly!

Snow angels made in giggle fits,
As our shapes drift, we toss and flit.
Shoveling paths leaves backs a'creak,
Yet through it all, we can only sneak.

In this canvas of white, so bright,
We laugh at our mess, oh what a sight!
Snowballs exchanged, and toasty bliss,
A day like this, who'd dare to miss?

Remnants of Autumn's Touch

Leaves still clung to frosty branches,
As snowflakes play in fleeting dances.
Birch trees shivering, dry leaves quiver,
Nature whispers as snowflakes deliver.

With scarves tied tight, we stroll out bold,
The chill recalls tales from the old.
Yet every gust makes us leap and squeal,
Battling the cold like it's a big deal.

Chestnuts roast to warm our hands,
While snowmen rise as winter stands.
Chocolate stains from tongue-tasting tricks,
Nature's palette gives us silly picks.

In this fluff, with laughter we cling,
To remnants of leaves, and the joy they bring.
A dance of colors now all turned white,
Yet here we are, all wrapped up tight.

Crystalline Echoes of the Past

Footprints map the tales we've spun,
In frosty dreams, it's always fun.
Giggles blend with winter's breath,
As we slide on ice, escaping death.

Frosty windows, art on display,
With little hands that find their way.
Snowflakes whisper secrets so sweet,
As we trip over hidden feet!

Echoes of laughter, lost in the air,
Chased by a snowball, beware, beware!
Each slip and slide a reason to bellow,
Only the snow can make us mellow.

In this icy waltz, we spin around,
Finding magic just off the ground.
A season of giggles, of slip, and of foot,
We'll cherish it all, our wintry hoot!

Shivers in the Twilight

Outside the snowflakes dance and play,
We trip and slide, what a clumsy ballet!
The nose turns red, the toes feel numb,
As we laugh, oh where did winter come from?

Hot cocoa spills, what a frothy mess,
Mittens mismatched, I must confess!
Sledding downhill, we scream with glee,
Then tumble over—who's the next to flee?

Icicles dangle like teeth on a grin,
We throw snowballs, aiming for kin!
But laughter erupts, as we all collide,
In this frosty world, there's no place to hide.

Frosty the snowman, with a carrot nose,
Melts in the sun, oh what a pose!
We wave goodbye, with a giggle and shout,
To the snowman's plight, we can't live without!

Enchantment of Frozen Dreams

The trees wear coats, all owlish and bright,
We fashion a hat, oh what a sight!
The dog in the snow looks like a bear,
Chasing his tail—oh, if we just care!

Slipping and sliding, we can't find our feet,
With woolen socks, we're not ready to greet.
Snowflakes land lightly, tickle our nose,
As laughter erupts; it's the best kind of prose.

A snowball fight breaks out in the park,
One little toss, then bingo—it sparks!
The war's now begun, but wait—pause in strife,
Uphill gets tricky, but hey, what a life!

Under the branches, we build a grand fort,
With icicles hanging, a frozen resort!
The world turns to spectacle, humor all around,
In this frosty adventure, we've all been unbound!

The Solstice's Breath

Jingle the bells, it's time to rejoice,
Skiing down hills with a gleeful voice!
But even the best can fall on their rear,
While winter just chuckles, oh dear, oh dear!

Snowmen in ties look quite dapper at best,
While snowball fights become quite the quest.
Hot tubbing outside in a blizzard we share,
Laughing it off, and we're unaware!

The icy pond beckons, it's time to glide,
With grace of a swan, or more like a slide!
But wait, where's my boot? Oh funnily lost,
In snowdrifts so deep, it's a snowman's frost!

The fire crackles, a warm bubble bath,
As visions of penguins start to dance with some math.
All bundled up tight, we swing and we sway,
In this jolly season, come laugh and play!

Crystalized Reflections

Beneath the stars, the world seems to giggle,
While icicles chime and the moon starts to wiggle.
In our puffy jackets and hats pulled down tight,
We sway as we dance in the soft, snowy night.

Snowball artillery, we've got quite the crew,
We pelt our friends, it's a slippery zoo!
With cheeks oh so rosy, the fun never ends,
Wistful reminders, oh how time bends.

Toasting to nights filled with laughter and cheer,
In our socks we prance, feeling free without fear.
Here's to the silliness that freezes the air,
With hearts full of warmth, winter's not so rare.

As we sit by the fire, let stories unfold,
With snowflakes now whispering the secrets they hold.
In this shimmering realm, where laughter's a spark,
We find joy in the chill, even when it gets dark!

Whispers from the Glittering Edge

The trees wear coats of chilly white,
Silly squirrels dance, what a sight!
They slip and slide on snow's soft floor,
Chasing each other, who could ask for more?

The ground's a canvas, sparkles abound,
Frosty flakes swirl, twirl around,
Snowmen grinning, they tip their hats,
As penguins laugh, let's play with the cats!

Hot cocoa spills, marshmallows roam,
Caught in the clutches of a frosty dome,
Icicles gleam like sharp candy canes,
Watch out! Here comes a snowball in lanes!

With every gust, the chill gets loud,
Even the snowflakes chuckle out proud,
Nature's joke, on us it plays,
We slip and giggle through frosty days!

Nature's Hoarfrost Lullaby

The world's wrapped tight in a frosty quilt,
Bunnies bounce 'neath the ice they've built,
Chasing their tails in a sparkling show,
Who knew critters could put on a glow?

The pond glistens, a frozen stage,
Where ice skates squeak, let's not disengage,
But Mrs. Duck takes a tumble down,
Her fluffed-up feathers make us all frown!

Tea kettles whistle, steam fills the air,
As snowflakes prance, it's quite the affair,
Pigeons in parkas, dapper and spry,
They strut like models, oh my, oh my!

With mittens on hands, we wave to the skies,
Giggling loudly at snowman's surprise,
His carrot nose starts to slide and sway,
Rolling down paths, what a silly day!

The Reflective Frost

A glimmering world made of ice and glass,
The ground's a mirror, but oh, we all pass,
Slipping and sliding, we flail and we spin,
Laughter erupts as someone falls in!

The sun peeks out, and what does it do?
Winks at the icicles, and they melt on cue,
Goofy little drips, a symphony of fun,
Each drop a giggle, oh what have we done?

Snowflakes twirl down, performing their dance,
Jumping on rooftops, they take a chance,
With scarves blowing wild, our hats take flight,
Chasing them down with squeals of delight!

Beneath all this frost, life's quite a show,
Even the cold has a warm, funny glow,
So here's to the season, for all its charms,
It tickles our hearts and keeps us from harms!

A Silent Hall of Winter's Echo

The wind giggles softly, a tickle in air,
Snow drips like honey, a sweet winter fair,
The blankets of frost wrap the world in light,
While ice-cream makers toil with delight!

Chubby little penguins waddle to chase,
As snowflakes giggle, it's a frosty race,
With every splash as they jump with glee,
Who knew that ice could be so silly?

Hot soup on the stove, bubbling away,
While snowmen chat and joke all day,
A carrot for noses, buttons for eyes,
They giggle together, what a big surprise!

So here's to the chuckles, the cold that we feel,
Nature's funny side with frosty appeal,
Dress up in layers, we're ready to play,
Let's warm up our hearts on this chilly day!

Shards of Winter's Whisper

Snowflakes tumble from the sky,
Each one lands with a silly sigh.
A snowman moans, he's way too cold,
His carrot nose is feeling bold.

Frosty breath in the morning light,
Dancing on rooftops, what a sight!
Penguins sliding, having a blast,
They race down hills, oh so fast!

Hot cocoa spills on my brand-new hat,
Guess I'll wear it, just like that!
Laughter echoes through the frozen air,
Winter's pranks, I have to beware.

With mittens big, I wave hello,
To a snowball fight, let's start the show!
A slip, a trip, and down I go,
These chilly times, a frosty glow!

The Glimmer of a Fading Day

The sun dips low in minty skies,
Snowmen stare with button eyes.
Sleds stacked high like a giant's hill,
Ready for trouble, what a thrill!

Icicles dangle, sharp as a spear,
One drops down, and I jump in fear!
A moose walks by with a snowball grin,
"Care to join?" Well, where do I begin?

With rosy cheeks and a frosty nose,
I toss like crazy, no time to doze.
Even the owl hoots with delight,
In this chilly dance, oh what a night!

When darkness falls, the air sings sweet,
With laughter echoing, it cannot beat.
The glow of the moon, it just won't stay,
As snowflakes chuckle, fading away!

Encased in Stillness

Everything pauses, the world holds breath,
As snow blankets all in chilly death.
Squirrels in jackets, looking so fine,
Dance on branches, to a nutty rhyme.

The trees are dressed in icy lace,
While birds refuse to leave their place.
A snowball flies, its aim is true,
But ducks just waddle, say, 'Not for you!'

Coffee cups freeze on the porch's edge,
As I make my way on the icy ledge.
Each step is cautious, a comedic slip,
Then a quick recovery, with a double flip!

I shout to the sky, "Why so frosty?"
The clouds giggle back, feeling quite lofty.
So here I stand, with friends so dear,
In this stillness, joy rings clear!

The Cool Caress of Twilight

Twilight sets like a frosted cake,
And ice on sidewalks, oh what a break!
I'm tiptoeing gingerly, just to be neat,
But gracelessly land on my own two feet!

Neighbors laugh from their windowed thrones,
As I make snow angels, mixed with groans.
A laugh-out-loud slip, it draws some cheers,
Ice skating mishap? Count it as gears!

The night creeps in, with whispers of fun,
Glistening lights, oh, what a run!
Dancing shadows beneath frosty trees,
I prance with my friends, all feeling at ease.

With jackets puffed and cheeks aglow,
We toast to the cute, and the chill we know.
In this twilight, where laughter flares,
I'm wrapped in joy, with snowy layers!

When Frost Meets the Hearth

The frost outside is quite the sight,
My toes are cold, but oh, what a night!
The cat's in a sweater, thinks he's so sly,
While I sip cocoa, and let out a sigh.

The fire crackles, hissing in glee,
Yet somehow it's cold as it can be.
Marshmallows dance, they think they're so grand,
But I can't feel my toes, oh, isn't it bland?

I toss in a log with a flick of my wrist,
But the room's still chilly, oh, what a twist!
A snowman's outside, looks just like my boss,
With eyes made of coal and a smile full of loss.

So here we sit, together we shiver,
My mug's getting empty, oh, how it quivers!
Tomorrow we'll laugh at this chilly charade,
As we bundle up tight in a warm little braid!

Frozen Footprints in Moonlight

Last night I ventured, with boots on my feet,
To catch the moon's glow, a beautiful treat.
But my toes went numb with each wobbly step,
Like a penguin on ice, I made quite the prep.

I traced little patterns, a twirl and a dash,
Until my own footprint caused quite the clash.
A slip and a tumble, oh, wasn't that fun?
My neighbors all laughed at my cold little run.

The snowflakes giggled, they danced on my head,
I swirled in confusion, then fell on my spread.
A snowman approached, said, "What a grand sight,
Let's dance in this moonlight, it'll surely feel right!"

So we boogied and glided, a pair so absurd,
Two frozen pals, not a single word.
But as dawn started creeping, I knew I must flee,
To thaw out my toes and drink pot after tea!

A Dance of Icicles

On the roof hangs a troupe, so quiet and sleek,
With each tiny drip, they practice their sneak.
They clink and they clatter, a melodious show,
While I stand below, dressed up like a snow.

I tiptoe about in my oversized gear,
Watching the icicles start to draw near.
One took a leap, but missed its soft crown,
It landed right on my head, oh, what a clown!

They skated on raindrops in a crystalline trance,
While I took a tumble, missing my chance.
With each frosty twirl, the world seemed to glow,
But my head sports a lump, oh, the price of the show!

So here I declare, with a chuckle and cheer,
Those icicles dance, but I'll stick to my beer.
We'll toast to the frosty, the funny and spry,
As the sun chases shadows in a soft, merry sky!

Embracing the Frostbound Dawn

Awake to a world wrapped in cold, white fluff,
With jammies still on, and my hair all a huff.
I shuffle to breakfast, a sight quite peculiar,
With crumbs on my chin, oh, what a great ruler!

The fridge greets me, with a chill and a wink,
As I ponder my coffee and recheck my drink.
Outside my window, I spot a bird freeze,
As it hops on the snow, looking too cute to tease.

I bundle up tight, with layers that bulge,
Like a marshmallow person intent to indulge.
But as I head out, I trip on my lace,
And land on my back, oh, it's a frosty embrace!

Yet laughter erupts as I roll in the cold,
With snowflakes atop me, a sight to behold.
So here I declare, in the frost's goofy glow,
Embracing the morning with laughter, let's go!

Echoes of the Snowfall

Snowflakes tumble down like actors in a show,
Diving from the roof, they put on quite a flow.
Lands in my cocoa, oh the frosty fun,
I sip and shiver; this should be a pun!

Snowmen wobble, is that a carrot nose?
Or just my neighbor's garden hosta in repose?
They dance in the wind, with arms made of sticks,
Stumbling like they've had too many pricks!

Sledding down the hill, my pants are now wet,
Last time I tried, but I'm not done yet!
A snowball fight breaks out in a flurry,
Turns out my aim's not great, oh what a worry!

But laughter fills the air, we're all feeling bold,
Though frozen fingertips are starting to fold.
Underneath the white, there lies a big joke,
In this cozy chaos, we'll never feel broke!

Serenity in Subzero

Icicles hang like teeth from the eaves,
Every time they tumble, my heart takes a heave.
The birds have left me, they're no longer here,
Guess they heard the rumors of frostbite and fear!

My hands are so cold, they might just break dance,
But I jiggle and wiggle, in this silly trance.
Polar bears in pajamas are roaming the street,
They wave and they shiver, now that's quite a feat!

The cat leaps from windows, a sprightly little fool,
Lands flat on her belly, oh what a cool duel!
One flake on her nose, she shakes it away,
Just like my hopes for warm sunshine today!

So here we are, wrapped in scarves so grand,
Stomping through snow, like we've lost our command.
Let's giggle and grin, 'till the thaw claims us all,
In this frosty delight, we'll have a ball!

Frostbitten Petals

In the garden, where flowers once bloomed in cheer,
Now they look frozen, in shock, oh dear!
Petals like cotton candy stuck in a freeze,
Even the bees took a long snooze with ease!

The sun comes out slowly, just a peek from the cloud,
But my toes are so numb, I'm far from proud.
Wearing mismatched mittens—blue but hey,
It's a fashion statement, or so I must say!

Pigeons hop along dressed in fluff and in glee,
Waddling like they've had one too many cups of tea.
One slips on the ice, and it's pure ballet,
The way it flails, brings laughter my way!

Though frosted and frozen, we'll find our delight,
With each silly stumble, and chuckle in sight.
For nature's great humor is here to unfold,
In this frozen realm, we're warm even in cold!

Beneath the Icebound Sky

Beneath this vast canvas of sparkling stars,
I slip and I slide, how silly are bars!
The moon gives a giggle as I take a fall,
Socks soaked with snow, I just won't recall!

The snowflakes whisper, a sneaky little tale,
Of penguins in top hats, oh how they regale!
They waddle and dance, with flair and finesse,
But here comes a snowball, my fluffy distress!

Gathered by fires, we sip cocoa hot,
While recounting the moments that could land us in a pot.

My friend claims they saw a worm doing a jig,
Turns out it was just my hat's newest gig!

So here's to the laughter, in this chilly delight,
As we navigate through the frosty moonlight.
With cold-nipped noses and hearts oh so free,
Let's embrace the giggles, together with glee!

A Frosty Oath of Serenity

In fluffy coats, we roam the street,
With noses red and frozen feet.
The snowflakes giggle, fall and swirl,
As we make snowmen, watch them twirl.

With sleds we race, we slip and slide,
The laughing snowball fights collide.
A friendly truce, a snowman's hat,
But wait, what's this? A furry cat?

Frost's Tender Caress

Cold fingers poke at frosty toes,
We build a fire, watch how it glows.
Hot cocoa spills upon my chin,
As marshmallows curl, they dance and spin.

On ice we glide with wobbly grace,
Like baby deer, we flail and chase.
Laughter echoes on the frozen lake,
"Who needs hot chocolate? It's a snowflake cake!"

Ripples in the Frozen Surface

Skating circles, 'round we go,
I'm dizzy now, look out below!
A slip, a fall, a giggly squeal,
"Next time we'll bring a heated wheel!"

The pond is frozen, but wait — it cracks!
With icy feet, we check our snacks.
"Did you bring lunch?" "Just snacks of air!"
With bellies grumbling, we sit and stare.

Wrapped in Crystal Clarity

The trees wear coats of sparkling white,
While squirrels scurry, what a sight!
A frosty breeze nips at our cheeks,
But oh, the warmth of laughter speaks.

With crystal glasses filled with cheer,
We toast to snowflakes swirling near.
A dance of joy, a frosty trance,
Who knew that snow could lead to chance?

The Frosted Embrace of the Earth

The ground wears a blanket, fluffy and white,
The snowflakes giggle, what a silly sight!
Snowmen are wobbling, hats a bit askew,
They fell on their noses, who's laughing? It's you!

Birds in the trees, they chirp and they squawk,
With frost on their feathers, they can hardly talk.
They dive for their seeds, all fluffy and round,
But slip with a flurry, and twist upside down!

Sleds slide like greased lightning down hills made of ice,
With laughter and chaos, who could be more nice?
A tumble and roll, with snow stuck in your hair,
Pajamas for snowpants? Who cares, we don't care!

So grab a hot drink, we'll giggle and play,
In this frosty wonderland, let's seize the day!
With cheeks all a-glow, and noses a bright red,
Let's toast to this madness, full hearts, brave and fed!

Sipping Cocoa by a Frosty Window

Sipping my cocoa, it's warm like a hug,
Outside it's a circus, a snowball snug!
With marshmallows dancing, floating on top,
I glance through the window and manage to hop!

The snowflakes tap-tap, a soft little rap,
They're telling me secrets, oh, where's my cap?
With each little flurry, the world turns so bright,
I'll join in the laughter, pretend it's a fight!

The cats are all tangled, caught in the yarn,
While snowmen are plotting to dance on the lawn.
With cocoa in hand, I take joy in the scene,
As I sharpen my aim, my snowballs are keen!

So cozy and chubby, I'll snuggle up tight,
What's this? Is that laughter I hear in the night?
With friends all around, this chill feels just right,
Let's raise our mugs high, to this frosty delight!

Frosted Whispers

Whispers of frost dance in the pale moonlight,
Laughter like icicles, a curious sight.
Snowflakes, like giggles, drift down from above,
They tickle my nose with a cold frosty shove!

The bunnies are hopping, all bundled and warm,
While icicles sparkle, they dance and they charm.
A squirrel in a sweater, it's quite the display,
Collecting his treasures, so foolishly gay!

Old boots left abandoned, lie flat in the snow,
Did someone forget them? Or did they just go?
With snowball ambushes from every side,
A flurry of laughter, can't take it in stride!

So come join the fun, in this frosty array,
With giggles and grins, we'll dance till the day.
The whispers of winter can't dampen our cheer,
For life's just much better with friends gathered near!

Chill of the Silent Night

The chill of the night creaks under our feet,
As snowmen are scheming, with plans oh so sweet.
The moon is a spotlight, bright on the stage,
Where penguins in bow ties perform with such rage!

The igloos are cozy, all snug and so round,
But watch for the snowflakes, they make quite a sound!
With shivers and giggles, we race through the white,
Chasing after snowballs that drift with delight!

Chinchillas in mittens, oh what a weird sight,
With snowflakes of giggles, they dance through the night.

Each snow-laden whisper brings joy to our hearts,
Frosty fun spills forth, oh where do we start?

So hold on to laughter, with hot cocoa near,
As we toast to this chill that brings laughter and cheer.
In the quiet of snow, let's conquer the day,
For joy's in the cold, let's merrily play!

White Silence and Shimmering Stars

In the quiet night we tread,
Snowflakes fall upon my head.
The ground's a blanket, soft and white,
I slip and slide, what a sight!

Snowballs flying through the air,
My hat's askew, not a care.
Laughter echoes, fills the scene,
Like a kid on a sugar bean!

Stars above begin to twinkle,
Underneath, we dance and crinkle.
Who knew falling could be fun?
We'll do it 'til the morning sun!

So let us sing, let us cheer,
With frosty noses, winter's here!
In this white world, we'll play like fools,
And defy all the chilly rules!

The Art of Stillness

In frozen air, our breath's a cloud,
We stand so still, feeling proud.
But here comes a sneeze, oh what a shock!
Down I go, like a rolling rock!

Frozen critters stare and laugh,
As I take my icy bath.
Penguins waddle past with glee,
While I flail 'round like a bumblebee!

Sipping cocoa, I find a chore,
My cup's now frozen to the floor!
Life's a joke in this chilly gust,
As we gather our warmth with trust!

So here's to stillness, let's remain,
In laughter, joy, and snowy gain.
We'll celebrate each frosty spill,
Cheers to life's cold and giggling thrill!

Beneath the Snow's Soft Veil

Beneath a shroud of feathery white,
I found a squirrel in my sight.
It's buried under all its loot,
Waking up to find a boot!

The trees are dressed, so snug and neat,
But watch your step, the ground's a treat!
One slip, and it's a comic fall,
Check your ego, once and for all!

Rabbits hopping, making tracks,
Their little footprints lead to snacks.
I'll leave a tip – bring carrots, friends,
Trust me, this fun never ends!

So let's embrace this frosty spell,
With giggles and jests, all is well.
For under layers cold and pale,
Life's funny games will always prevail!

Lanterns Glowing in the Chill

Lanterns flicker, casting light,
On shoes that slip—a comical sight!
Hear the laughter, soft and bright,
As snowmen wobble in the night!

With my scarf wrapped snug and tight,
I trip and tumble—what a plight!
But every fall just brings a cheer,
For laughter's warmth is always near!

Hot soup awaits, steam in the air,
While frozen fingers tug at hair.
I'll juggle snowballs if you dare,
But watch the splash; beware, beware!

So let us revel, make no haste,
With snowflakes swirling, life's a taste.
For in this chill, though we may freeze,
A giggle warms better than cheese!

Beneath the Frosted Canopy

Icicles hanging, they giggle and sway,
Telling us jokes from the cold, snowy play.
Snowflakes that dance with a frosty delight,
Whispering secrets in the hush of the night.

Beneath the white quilt, the squirrels do prance,
In fluffy white jackets, they twirl and they dance.
With cheeks full of acorns, they laugh and then slide,
On patches of ice where the brave ones confide.

The blanket of snow brings out penguin styles,
As bunnies hop by in their fur-lined big smiles.
Cartwheeling snowmen with noses of carrots,
Tell funny old tales that no one ever inherits.

So let winter rain down with a chill and a chuckle,
For beneath the frost, our hearts huddle and snuggle.
With laughter and joy in the shimmering freeze,
We find warmth in the chaos, a life full of ease.

Tapestry of Frost and Light

The trees wear their crystals, a glittering crown,
While the sun peeks through, making snowflakes dance down.
A frosty parade with a wink and a spin,
As we chuckle at how winter always takes a win.

Frosty windows draw pictures of goofy old bears,
Who slide on the ice with the grace of old chairs.
Each step turns to slip, it's a comical show,
As we laugh at our tumbles, with cheeks all aglow.

With breaths steaming like dragons, we gather for fun,
Making snowdogs and snowcats until we are done.
A tapestry woven with laughter and cheer,
In a land where each snowman holds secrets to share.

So raise up your mugs, let the joy overflow,
For the blanket around us is more than just snow.
It's the warmth of our giggles, the joy that we find,
In a place where the cold's never frostbitten our mind.

Secrets of the Frostkissed Dawn

The dawn breaks in shimmers, a quirky delight,
With rays tickling snowflakes, all frosty and bright.
Penguins play hopscotch on ice patches low,
While the rabbits just giggle at the clumsy show.

A chilly secret waits in the soft morning light,
A snowman's long story of his frosty night fright.
His carrot for a nose points to mischief untold,
As the squirrels plot pranks and the rabbits grow bold.

They build up tall castles, a kingdom of fluff,
But each royal decree ends in laughter, not tough.
Snowball fights erupt like a wintery blast,
With giggles and snow showers, a season that's vast.

So gather near fires, let the chuckles resound,
For the secrets of dawn are where humor is found.
In a realm full of ice, let's find reasons to play,
And weave threads of laughter throughout the cold day.

The Solitary Pine

The solitary pine stands tall and quite proud,
Wearing crystals like jewels in a shimmering shroud.
With branches that tickle the sky up above,
He sways to the whispers, a dance full of love.

Around him, the critters, in coats of bright white,
Share jokes in the shadows of long winter nights.
With squirrels telling tales of the nuts that were lost,
And rabbits sharing giggles at the terrible frost.

Each flake brings a chuckle as it lands on his head,
The pine wears a hat that the blustery made.
He chuckles out loud, with a bough-happy grin,
With laughter the promise of mischief to spin.

So here's to the pine, in his icy attire,
Bringing fun to the gloom as our hearts burn like fire.
In a world of cold wonder, let's raise a warm cheer,
For the joy that he spreads as the season draws near.

Secrets Wrapped in Ice

A snowman with a top hat laughs,
His button eyes hold secret gaffs.
In winter's chill, we hide and tease,
While penguins slide with careless ease.

Icicles dangle like silly swords,
While snowballs fly, defying the cords.
We slip and slide on the frozen ground,
In this quirky world, laughter's found.

The dog prances in boots too tight,
Chasing flakes, a comical sight.
Snowflakes tickle our noses red,
As we all dance, quite misled.

With cocoa mugs, we toast the cold,
To frosty tales that never grow old.
In this chilly realm, we laugh so bright,
Secrets wrapped in snow, pure delight.

Glacial Breath of Night

The moon winks at the frozen stream,
Casting shadows that giggle and gleam.
Snowmen whisper secrets so sly,
While a daring rabbit pops by.

Starry flakes tumble, a shimmering show,
As our frosty breath dances with snow.
We build a fort, hide inside,
Using snowballs for those playful rides.

A grumpy cat in a snow-speckled coat,
Watches from inside, won't take a vote.
Squeaky boots and snow-tipped hats,
Each step sounds out like a chorus of chats.

As the clock strikes, we say, 'Oh dear!'
Laughing as we slip, full of cheer.
In the glacial breath of this night divine,
We'll spin tales that sparkle and shine.

Shadows in the Snow

Footprints dance like shadows low,
In the crisp white blanket, we twirl and flow.
The snowflakes giggle, swirl, and dive,
As we take turns trying to survive.

Beep beep! A sled rushes down the hill,
With squeals of joy, we chase the thrill.
A tumble here, a giggle there,
In frosty fun, we haven't a care.

Hot cocoa calls from the cabin's glow,
With tiny marshmallows all in a row.
While mittens huddle, warm in a clump,
Making snowmen, we all take a jump.

The night falls softly, we can't resist,
Building snow forts, we laugh and twist.
In shadows of snow, we create our scene,
With friends and giggles, life feels serene.

The Heart's Thaw in Frost's Hold

When frost decorates the world all around,
Our hearts feel light, unbound and unbound.
Winter games bring joy to our day,
As laughter dances and snowflakes play.

A squirrel in sunglasses, oh what a sight,
Stealing our snacks, a comical bite.
With snowball fights that spiral and fly,
While giggles echo beneath the grey sky.

Snowsuits squeak, we tumble and roll,
Chilling escapades warm the soul.
A hot chocolate toast, cheers fill the air,
Our hearts defrost, melting all care.

As dusk settles down, we gather to share,
Stories of snowmen and how they declare.
In frost's hold, with mischief and cheer,
The warmth of our hearts draws us near.

Threads of Cold in Darkened Skies

In frosty air, we dance around,
With mittens on, we trip and sound.
The snowflakes fall like tiny stars,
While we throw snowballs from afar.

Our noses red, we laugh and tease,
An ice rink's fate brings us to knees.
Yet in the chill, we find our cheer,
With frozen eyebrows, no need for fear.

The squirrels scurry, little blurs,
Dressed in coats, they're such good spurs.
We mimic them and leap in play,
While snowmen watch us on display.

But as the cold sets in its grip,
We dance with frost; we take a dip.
Oh, what a sight this merry spree,
In chilly joy, forever free.

When the World Pauses to Freeze

As snowflakes touch upon the ground,
The world stands still; no hopeful sound.
We slip and slide, grasping for hand,
Each tumble's worth a laugh so grand.

The tea is brewing, warmth is near,
Yet outside, chaos reigns with cheer.
With every gust that flutters by,
We seek a laugh, not a goodbye.

Frozen fingers make us fumble,
But who can resist a snowy tumble?
Life's little slips bring us delight,
Let's giggle at the frosty bite.

So come, my friends, let's roam the streets,
In laughter's glow, our joy repeats.
For when the world stands still in frost,
It's joy we find, not what is lost.

Muffled Laughter Amidst the Flurries

In fluffy lands where giggles hide,
The snowy hills become our slide.
With sleds and bones, we take the jump,
And land with grace, a floppy thump.

Wooly hats just won't keep still,
As snowballs fly, it's such a thrill.
The laughter echoes, muffled yet bright,
With frozen cheeks, we glow with light.

As snowmen rise with carrot-nose,
We draw mustaches and strike a pose.
Each gentle flake, a teasing wink,
Chasing hot cocoa at the brink.

And when it's time to head back home,
With frosted eyes, we'll stop and roam.
For laughter keeps the chill at bay,
In snowy realms, we'll gladly play.

Nestling Within Piles of Snow

In blankets soft of snowy white,
We burrow deep, oh what a sight!
With chubby cheeks and giggling sounds,
Our cozy forts become our grounds.

The world outside is cold and drear,
But in my nest, we hoot and cheer.
Hot cocoa's slipping through my hands,
As laughter spills like golden sands.

We throw a tiny snowball fight,
With laughter soaring, pure delight.
A fort of dreams in chilly air,
Creating joy, beyond compare.

So, come and join this snowy scene,
Where joy's the goal, and smiles are keen.
Snuggled warm in winter's play,
We find the funny in each day.

Milton Keynes UK
Ingram Content Group UK Ltd.
UKHW022011131124
451149UK00013B/1103